the

second

blush

the
second
blush

POEMS

Molly Peacock

W. W. Norton & Company   NEW YORK · LONDON

For information about permission to reproduce selections from this book,
write to Permissions, W. W. Norton & Company, Inc.,
500 Fifth Avenue, New York, NY 10110

For information about special discounts for bulk purchases, please contact
W. W. Norton Special Sales at specialsales@wwnorton.com or 800-233-4830

Manufacturing by Courier Westford
Book design by Chris Welch
Production manager: Julia Druskin

Library of Congress Cataloging-in-Publication Data

Peacock, Molly, date.
The second blush : poems / Molly Peacock. — 1st ed.
p. cm.
ISBN 978-0-393-06651-7 (hardcover)
1. Middle age—Poetry. 2. Marriage—Poetry. I. Title.
PS3566.E15S43 2008
811'.54—dc22

2008001500

W. W. Norton & Company, Inc.
500 Fifth Avenue, New York, N.Y. 10110
www.wwnorton.com

W. W. Norton & Company Ltd.
Castle House, 75/76 Wells Street, London W1T 3QT

1 2 3 4 5 6 7 8 9 0

For Michael Groden

Contents

i.

ii.

iii.

iv.

i.

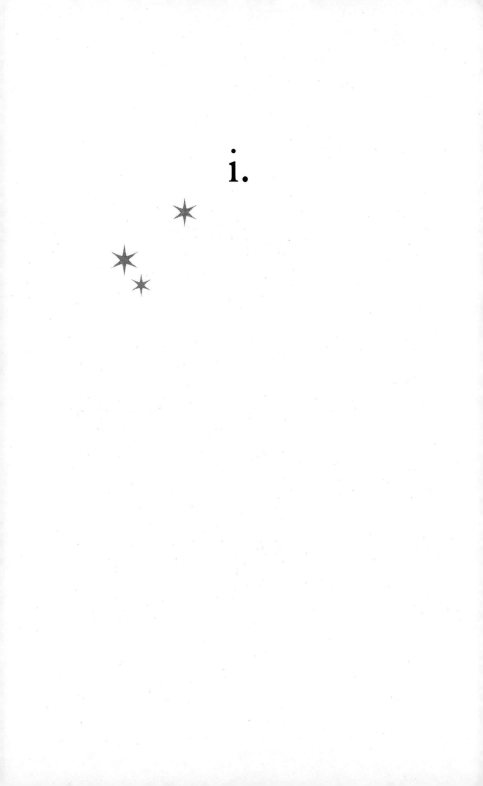

Of Night

A city mouse darts from the paws of night.
A body drops from the jaws of night.
A woman denies the laws of night,
awake and trapped in the *was* of night.
A young man turns in the gauze of night,
unraveling the cause of night:
that days extend their claws at night
to reenact old wars at night,
though dreams can heal old sores at night
and spring begins its thaw at night,
while worry bones are gnawed at night.
He sips her through a straw at night.
Verbs whisper in the clause of night.
A finger to her lips

                      the pause of night.

The Happy Diary

¶ A man on the train feeding grapes to his son.*
¶ Tossing my shoes in the trash one by one.
¶ The smell of tomato sauce. ¶ Square of sun.
(*THE BOY SLIPPED THE GRAPES IN HIS MOUTH ONE BY ONE.)
¶ Deciding NEVER AGAIN and being really done.
¶ Feeling the change as drawn lines become
a road through a field. ¶ Fresh clear water run
from an unused pump. ¶ Making a pun un-
expectedly. ¶ Out of the oven, on
the table, on time. ¶ A bet finally won.
¶ Unlocking the door, exhausted—the tongue
wakes up at the smell of pesto. ¶ Plumb
walls and doors. ¶ Also, plums.
                              I put each one
in the Happy Diary, which I started one
day, when I was undone.

The Silver Arrow

With your fifteen percent chance to survive,
marriage seemed a doomed possibility,
yet melanoma taught us to live
on two tracks with two new velocities:
Track Death—with cancer fantasies, ~~life~~
without ~~you~~, without ~~us~~ —and *Track Future*
—track of speed, of world detritus, of wife.
Wife of gold and dirt. What won't/will occur.
Husband of the steady beat. Our joke in bed:
we married for security! We rode
The Silver Arrow into probability,
piercing a landscape that rumpled into hills instead
of tarred plains. Fifteen years to love and rove
unbidden, through the forbidden city.

Our Xanadu

Inside the forbidden city no one
stops us. Since we have managed to get here,
we must have a right to the opaline sun
and the outdoor staircase that appears
just when we want to descend to the next
level, toward the hidden garden.
Lintels pop out of nowhere—context
is threshold after threshold here in the Arden
of the interior where the sea laps at our feet
though we stand on the dry cobbled street.
Up above, instead of birds,
the slow motion spitfire of killing words
patterns the sky. In another atmosphere,
far, far away, death becomes an air show—
—but we are safe a moment, looking up from below.

Faraway

I could lose you, but I haven't so far.
I might amuse you, but I daren't, so far.
I could confuse you, but I won't, so far.
Would I refuse you? *No,* I say.

I've chosen you, yes, this far
from where I was born, far away
from where I woo you, using my hands

to soothe you, meeting your hands.
Now our fingers smooth out the view
as if we're stretching a canvas of a landscape
back onto the land itself—but too big! but too far—

we dive under its contours, everything blurs,
then you drop a clue,
                          and the land reshapes;
I pick it up,
              and we pull through,
                                      so far.

Good Fortune

A braceletted wrist with a good luck charm,
its hand on a cup of coffee resting
calmly in the handle's curl (no questing),
finger and thumb out of the way of harm
(no jesting, either), digits in command
of their nervous system, system of veins,
of their muscles and tiny bones—that hand
about to raise the cup, the bracelet chains
rattling against the tender wrist, up, up
—and in the rise, a tiny man inscribed
on the good luck charm begins to get up
from his lotus pad and put on his shoes.
Now the contents of the cup will be imbibed,
and the day will begin with something to lose.

The Cliffs of Mistake

To know you're making a mistake as
you make it, yet not be able to stop,
is to step off a cliff, expecting to scramble
backward and up through the air to stand
on the outcrop you stepped from,
even though it can't unhappen as you
backpeddle wildly with the second step,
looking far, far below onto the moraine
of pain you anticipate later, which is now
only the shock of recognizing the result
there's no leaping back from.
Oh God, and this is only a metaphor.
Might this be what metaphors are for?
To say what it's like
                    before you hit what it is.

The Cup

Unable to quell a sudden urge for neatness,
I reached to put away my Summerhouse cup,
lifting up a wire shelf insert by mistake,
rolling a whole stack of china toward me,
barefoot in my nightgown on a step stool,
dropping the precious cup, which smashed
as I pushed both my hands to save the rest
—and did.
             I tried not to make too much
of the one I'd never lift to my lips,
throwing the pieces out immediately.

        It's only a cup,
        You saved the rest.

Oh yes, I did, but just as in a classroom
where all the pupils quietly work but one who refuses,
my mind roves to an unlearning I mourn
even as I see the stacks
of all that has been accomplished—and saved.
Why couldn't I have just had breakfast
before I started my tasks?

Because he was a flushed and violent boy
I had not thought of in twenty years
until his mother wrote me he had died,
not saying the cause,
and I cannot say the boy was the cause of my urge,
a sweaty boy caught hanging the shorter kids
up by their collars on the high coatroom hooks
and whose ruddy face looked so little like porcelain.

Ferocity in a Dishpan

Into the dish suds a wineglass falls,
shattering as it jostles the other things.
The young woman—the dish doer—
picks the big pieces out, sets them on the range,
never emptying the dishwater—why bother?—
and ends up slicing a shark-mouthed flap
into her little finger, blood everywhere.
Over the keyboard my fingers fly
then pause, at the sight of my hands:
now the old scar is deeper! I wonder why
it didn't fade, as scars are supposed to.
Is it because I've never learned better?
Just to keep going, as if it didn't matter . . .
because existence depends on ardor?

Picnic

As we pack up our picnic dishes,
lake-tired, dreamy, we notice two cygnets,
almost the size of their parents,
flanking the grown swans diving for fish.
The whole way back we keep them in our eye
as we tote our trash and blanket. Almost grown.
About the age, in swan-years, that we were
when we met. Dawdling, we stop to buy
a dusty cantaloupe, its rind pocked and lobed.

We met at the age when we questioned
everything, though now to probe
the universe for our fortune
might end the ease of this hour,
a watching so satisfying it's exhausting:
boat sails rising, as if out of battle fog . . . the blue
draining unexpected pockets of old worries
as the swan flotilla of childhood recedes. . . .

We cut into the cantaloupe when we get home,
but it's not memory, and it's not war,
it's just a rough globe grown on a vine,
and we're delighted, as we always are,
to bite the orange beneath its dome.

Pink Paperclip

A pink plastic paperclip lies prone on
the counter, its curve-return-curve
out of reach of the dishcloth: I miss it
as I swipe the crumbs into the trash
with my ruthless urge to order.
My husband comes by, saying
"I've got a foster home for paperclips,"
and takes it to his room, to a little box
where it waits in readiness,
the color of a girl's barrette.
I might have chucked it,
and this is why the gods terrify me.
Yet they merely interest him, among all
the other beings in the world, including me,
whom he still finds useful,
even inspiring my new goal:
to personify everything,
each in the bloom of its use,
becoming a poet after all.

Confession

I confess to my husband
all my little sins:

I was mean
I was petty

This happened
That happened.

You had to do it, he says.
Or else he confounds me,

asking his questions,
all I'd never thought of.

Why is it a poem
to confess to one's husband?

Am I that mere thing,
a confessional poet?

My confessions are artless
because they are desperate,

but the poem shines
like a heart exposed.

I haven't bothered
to tell you my sins—

You're not my husband.
(*Thank God,* you say),

you're my reader—
but have you ever read a poem

where a husband
is a confessor?

Not veiled in a booth,
but a seeker after truth.

Not in a collar,
but in his sweatpants

unshaven, tousled
not much to you, reader

but to me
shining like a leaf

in the after-rain sun
beaded with a jewel

that's merely
a water drop.

ii.

The Match

From an inner courtyard of a Dublin flat
late at night rose two voices, a woman's
and a man's, keeping a narrow balance
that seesawed from boast to accusation.
I never heard the words as I stood,
wakened, by the window,
only the tone-swords of the drunken parry:
silence, then thrust, foe-to-beloved-foe
that one jab could unbalance,
but they were matched—so far.

Fifty years peeled back as I heard the voices
of my mother and father, not the words,
but a tone bar raising and lowering,
choices calibrated to the tip of violence,
and felt the panic of suspension between them
like driving toward another car on a bridge,
with no chance to swerve,
about to be thrown to oblivion.
                              Yet behind me,
thrown back by my husband in his solid sleep,
lay the swerve of our sheet's white hem.

Blasphemy & Blame

On Pearse Street in Dublin I saw a man
and a woman—short, squat, red-faced and drunk—
screaming at each other in the August sun,
and all I had built, the pillars I thought I'd sunk
into a new foundation, became matchsticks
blown aloft over the ugly street. That man,
egged on by the woman, would get his licks
in soon, I knew, though my calm husband
hardly noticed them. Then my beloved,
my pillar, like paper, began to catch flame,
edges curling with blasphemy and blame,
flying beside me, then aloft, near
then away. No hand to hold dear.
That couple? My dead parents twinned.
My husband? Taken off by the wind.

In the Winter Dark

We walk alone toward the car on the street
as two men loom, young, arguing, drunk.
A blown out street lamp blocks the door
on the passenger side, my side.

My husband, barely aware of the men
waving two open bottles, walks to his side
and gets in behind the wheel. I face them,
and as one turns toward us I flatten,

then slip around the car to the street
through the rear door as if my husband
were a taxi driver and scream,
"Lock the doors and drive!"

He hasn't even turned the ignition yet.
I start to freeze in cold fury,
but something seeps into me like dry gas
fueling forward motion

as my mild husband
eases the car into traffic, saying,
"Oh those party guys, they're
only focused on themselves."

Small Fry

A fish I'd become, dragged up in a net:
one tear hung at the corner of my eye.
Crowded at the dock (the foot of the bed)

my ancestors milled, smelling of wet wool,
wet capes, caps, bonnets, vests, and a smell
of oil on the pulley ropes of the grappling hooks

of the ships where they loaded their sheep,
and the oil on the gears of a clock
cranking backward through the centuries.

"Our flesh hallowed in your flesh,"
they said, surprised as I was to meet them
fish to face through a loop in the net.

"My living cells in yours," I said.
Later on that day when it was bright
and they'd gone away, I'd press on alone,

but this night we met at the shore.
The smell of fish and sheep became the smell of sleep.
Then they threw me back into the twisted sheets.

The Blanket

Antarctica

I woke to the voice of my dead sister.
She was *cold,* she said, colder than she'd
ever been in life. Eight years dead—freed
from being used by our father, or so
I thought until I heard her.

                    You by the door,
ready to leave this poem, stay with me.
Here I am demanding that you listen
as she asks that I listen from beyond.
She had no choice. (That is living death, isn't it?)
Antarctica, the place without choice.

                            Why,
why are you still down there? I call,
Haven't you been reborn by now?
Turned back to a blonde eight-year-old
tumbling down a hill . . .

                    Oh reader,
excuse me. I have presumed on you
once again. Can't you help me
heave the heavy lid of this chest
and lift the blanket out? Help me
toss it down to the end of the world.

The End of the World

Snapping out like whipcrack in the cold
the loose harness slapped against the sleigh,
while the three of them marched beside the runners,
snow to the horizon, and in the dead bright cold
the magnified clop of the hooves of their horse
followed behind them. Their mother'd decided
to give the steed a rest, so they set a dogged
swish-pace with their snowshoes, a course
somehow determined by the woman—she
knew the way—although before them was nothing
but a blank snowfield, and behind them their horse,
coat grown as woolly as a fairy-tale pony, plodding
while the two young girls trudged into nothing,
blinded by the snow-sea.
They were colder than they'd ever been or ever would be.
No tree. No winter hare or straggler army
came across them, and yet they pushed on, stunned,
the mother heaving her bulk against the sleigh,
and on the seat their refuge of skins abandoned.

The Throne

When I was afraid, fear took me in,
and gave me a cold seat in her kingdom
from which I looked for all my kin
and found no mother, no father. Dumb
I was, and deaf then. Touch only I had,
only the cold claws of the chair arms did
I feel, and hollowness in my head.
My mother was dead. My father was dead.
I gripped the throne of fear with my right hand,
and the seat of the chair held me upright
or I would have fallen. I couldn't stand.
But the throne's left arm was warm with human might.
It took my hand and held me in its own,
that the kingdom of fear might be overthrown.

Little Scar

The twin nature of a wound is healing
and reminding. The same scar that means
"it's over" recalls that the hard dead spot
at its center was once alive to feeling.
People worry about remembering
as they push aside what remains,
as if "getting over it" made the thought
of what happened into an obstacle,
but anyone who's lost anything, even
a torn stuffed bear, knows loss is the vestibule
to a parallel universe inside grieving,
where all who were lost still seem living.
Now we have to live with a scar, a strange
benumbed place we reenter as we change.

iii.

Girl and Friends View Naked Goddess

after Pier Celestino Gilardi's painting A Visit to the Gallery

She'd rather be nude, she'd rather be dressed,
rather cover up her bum and breasts.
If she dropped her clothes would she look like *this*?
A sculpted goddess, bare as an almond?
Her girlfriends buzz about those goddess tits,
though the shy one stares straight ahead—stunned
to see what she might become. What might
the goddess become if she could untighten
her gaze and be part of her watchers' scene?
Ruffled, laced, stockinged and corsetted,
this girl's dying to shed it all; a sheen
of longing on her face asks, "Can't I be rid
of my stays?" But the object she'd become
would have to stay in the hall alone

in the clammy gloom of every Roman night. . . .
Goddess, her ideal, may you not feel
or have to possess a soul. . . . Let that light
inside these girls, who'll dash down the hall
with arms linked, out for a bite to eat and
lots of gossip at their visit's end
(for now they've seen her, and she's inside them,
a man's ideal, and they see they could be she,
the naked lady of a sculptor's whim,

cold as the floors they walk on), let that light glow.
May they dress up daily, may their servants stir
hot washtubs of bloody cotton strips to insure
they won't bleed on their taffetas. May they laugh
at a man inserting his soul in a sculpture.

May the sculpture not feel it intrude there,
and chafe. And may her observers have futures.

Drawing for Absolute Beginners

Why was I there in that museum basement,
my arm and leg asleep in their cramped positions?
I would never draw the oval, nab the shadow, find the texture—
what could I do to soothe my frenzy of inability?
My clever classmates all got busy
while my muse turned into a schoolmarm:
Now, look, there's a brown egg the shape of a plum.
It's the simplest shape in the world.
It begs to be drawn!
But when I looked down I saw
ten thousand miles to simplicity
and shivered.

                    I thought of Bartleby. I preferred not to.
I shoved my muse into his sweater, and we fled
into below-zero weather, drove to our apartment complex
where the orchids I'd wanted to draw
lolled above the frozen city, complex
and mystifying. *What's next?* my muse said,
after he had his tea and a cookie.
"I can barely follow them with my eye,
let alone with my pencil!"
Let us try.

Great-Grandmother's Young Ghost

*H*er rocking chair sails the living room:
*E*ternity makes sense when the runners rock,
*R*iding the blue braided rug as a flume,
*R*ocking a sea of floorboards pocked
*O*ver and over by heels of a century
*C*arving their emphasis into the floors,
*K*nocking the years into waves that now crash
*I*nto shores—the oaken arms the oak of oars.
*N*othing can be put behind her fury
*G*rinding the waves. How far from the wall her
*C*hair must be battened—its slender shape, like
*H*er hair, flings wildly as it rocks, all
*A*ir bestirred. If you try her chair, life crashes
*I*ts way through the frumious
*R*olling as if, through you, she's there.

Gargoyle

Sheela na Gig, lady on her haunches,
squats with arms down, pulling her pudenda
away from her clitoris, which launches
out of her stone sculpted body a
prow that even when wind and hail blast a-
way her dugs and ribs and ears and bald head
snorks past any dilemma
of what it is: sex flung wide above a
church door, a masturbating gargoyle wed
to worship, her bulging eyes popping in
an orgasm, or death, or warning, or in
the puckered surprise of the release of
her god inside—old, old among the folds. Of
wraith-wisdom this: self-love.

Artichoke Heart

Every time I cook an artichoke I
think of you—you taught me. Every time I
pay too much for a plump cutlet I hear
your praise-in-disapproval (you'd steer
toward something with the bone in). Now pastry,
those two sexes of Sicilian pastry:
penises (you'd point at a baba), or
female (pointing to that crusted butterfly d'or
next to it). That was certainly true of
us. Every minute we were aware of
the biology of our lovers' differences.
Our kind of breakup doesn't mend fences,
so I have not called you up the hundreds
of dinner times I've thought of you. Instead,
I've prepared an artichoke head.

The Fly

I asked her for a favor, and
felt the wing of her Yes.
When it was time for the favor to be done,
she buzzed, "I'm in need of one myself."
But mine hadn't been given yet!
This was cashing in before you pay.
Instead I incurred a debt far greater
than what I asked to borrow.
What made me so blind? In sunlight,
a housefly has landed on my knee.
Its garnet eyes are so pretty.
Here I thought she liked me for myself.
How little I know of how human beings work.

Fellini the Cat

He bit me before he died, then hissed
at the vet who shaved his paw for the prick
of the euthanasia needle she'd stick
into a vein while we held him. Then she kissed
his dead nose as we touched him. His spirit
hadn't really had a chance to leave yet,
his green eyes wide open, not all shut
in pain like the last hours—*Would we like to have
a souvenir of his fur?* she asked. *Oh yes,*
we said, and a moment later she'd shaved
two swaths off the wild field of his thin coat,
a shock only a blanket up to his neck could redress.

The Pearl Tear

In the white of your eye I see
a speck's flown in. Now a seed pearl's forming.
The irritant has stuck. You can't get free
of it, nor can the speck undo the storming
tissue that wraps around it,
soft with tears at first, then hard with lustre.
Oh my dear, I wonder when you cry will it
slip down your cheek, and will you, flustered,
brush the pearl away with the back of your hand?
And if it lands nearby, will you notice it?
Will you pick it up, marvel, and thread it
onto a string of threats you've empearled?
Or will you ignore it, failing to understand,
and bare your neck again to the world?

Widow

Home from the vet, she sniffed the usual
corners, knew instantly the male was gone
and began to purr so loudly the dull
interpretation of purring as con-
tentment proved bleak and wrong: this was keening.
She put her head beneath my hand, leaning
all her weight into it, and when I let
go finally, she followed me to the
bathroom, climbed on my lap on the toilet,
followed me to the bed, to the sink, the
closet where she flopped her fifteen years' weight
down in the dark, and prepared to wait.

Old Friends

One waiting, one attending. Patience.
Now a gift will be delivered. Her food
from her hands. Her turn tonight. All the good
little dishes assembled and friendship hence
ever so slightly adjusted in level.
No one grows evenly. One surges. One lags.
But here comes a resting point. All
focus on a platter: two sole almost wag
their tails, so happy are they to be served.
Lovely. Think so? Thank you. Our pleasure
crosses and recrosses, making cursive
loops as if written on paper, a measure
of lines made by our lives as they swerve by
making letters. My meal. Her meal. A missive.

Ghost Cat

Back behind the hanging shoe bag.
Beside the box of old diplomas.
On the half-shelf by the phones.
Below the scanner, on the plastic bag.
Pass the clothes hamper—only socks and T-shirts.
A quick bulge in the curtains flirts
with the windowsill, then lies still.
Between the cabinet and table,
a jump down to the lid of the cardboard box
where I'm not supposed to see.
Only a piece of chewed crochet. TV cable.
Why isn't she there?
Only the clocks. Only air.
Check the windowsill. The sunspot bare.

The Rescuer

Certain people take huge pride in keeping
others alive, and I was one of these.
Rescuing, to me, meant suddenly leaping
out of my mind and landing on those
whom I thought I should help like a panther
—a sleek shadow-thing with a rippling hide
and a growl covered by a purr.
But even as I coaxed the needy to my side,
I realized that having leapt from my mind
meant I was lost. (To anyone who'd listen
I declared, "I must be out of my mind!")
Way beyond my jungle other minds glistened,
pearl-like as flowers in rich park loam
tended by those who love their jobs, but go home.

Vision in the Backseat of a Taxi

As she flung the insult, she saw my face
and apologized as our taxi lurched
into traffic—"Not my finest moment."
Then I looked down to find my minor wound
healing, even as I laid eyes on it,
moving through stages of the fresh cut, blood
coagulating, a scab forming (as if
a child had fallen and gashed her knee,
then watched it mend in fast-forward motion).
I forgot her, close by my side,
too busy marveling at my rapid recovery,
until I turned to see her face almost completely
covered in pus, a wound opened again,
attempting to repair: the yellow-green cells
summoned after each slur splattered back
like pan grease from a fire far away
from the moist day we rattled through the city
with our taxi window open.
By the time we bumped downtown,

even my scar had faded
as if all the years I lived had erased it.
Then we heaved out of the sagging seat and
opened the battered yellow door onto
the dusty road
that ancient Philip of Macedonia traveled,
saying, Lo, each traveler you meet
carries a great burden.

Teacup Manifesto

Bivouacked in a woman's living room,
a heap of soldiers, dusty as flour sacks,
sleeps on her carpet. Will the woman ever
return to beat those crimson fibers free of their
sifting particles? The slanted teacup tower
in her cabinet behind them must tremble
every time a soldier groans or turns.
The ridged wool of the carpet against their cheeks
makes creases they'll have to rub from their faces,
when they tear off the webs of sleep.
Probably none of the teacups will survive.
(The boy's gloves look so thick they might
not even be able to pick one up. . . .)
The teacups slightly gasp from the seepage of dust.

Long, long from this January day and
the photograph I have tumbled into,
in a hypnagogic moment between sleep,
the new cats' cries, and the filling of the teakettle,
perhaps a museum case will be unlocked,
and a twisted fiber from her carpet, labeled
and numbered, laid next to a classified shard
(one of her cups). From this someone

will be obliged to imagine an entire civilization.
Armpit rot, crotch rot, and the rank smell of sleep
let the boys steep the tea of their dreams,

while my husband, so much older than these kids,
lies drenched in a fever, curled up in our bed
and, in the boundary-less anxiety of the kettle steam,
I worry equally about the lost woman not
on the front of the newspaper, and him,
and the boys. The still photo comes alive
and they thrash, raw, curling into each other
as my husband curls—and as the metal
cocking of the cat food can brings
the animals to swarm their saucers,
I cleave to the unformed idea that
it must be cups men fight for.
The chance to wake in a sweat and drink
from something that claims a moment of peace
just because it could break.

iv.

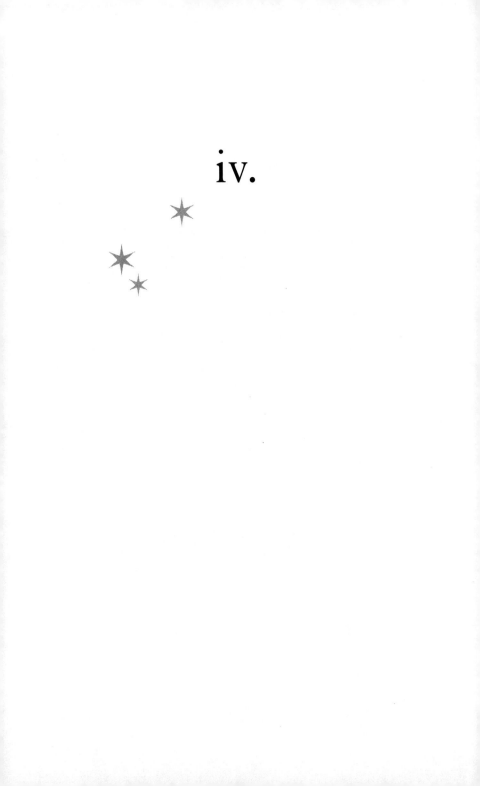

Chance

may favor obscure brainy aptitudes in you
and a love of the past so blind you would
venture, always securing permission,
into the back library stacks, without food
or water because you have a mission:
to find yourself, in the regulated light,
holding a volume in your hands as you
yourself might like to be held. Mostly your life
will be voices and images. Information. You
may go a long way alone, and travel much
to open a book to renew your touch.

Intuition

When the senses fleur—taste buds, fingertips,
a flicker in the corner of the lips—
something so quick, so low, then very slow,
something you don't even know you know
wakens a reception you don't know you have,
until you start to deny it. You might even have
to protect yourself from it, if you've been
shutting yourself off from the unseen
since childhood. But this is the real adventure
of adulthood: mere indenture to fact
finally reaches its limit, and you can act
without looking, pricking your ears to the sound
no one else seems to hear through the air
but you, all on your own.

The Vow

Every time you suffer disappointment
it makes me fall in love with you again
because I almost cannot bear to see
the dumbstruck purity in your face bent
on figuring how or why you couldn't see
it coming. *Maybe I could have fixed it when*
things were in the planning stage, but now
that it's turned out so badly, you say, *what*
can we do? I fall in love with the valence
of your chemistry rebalancing.

                      Valiance
is an animal virtue I learn again as you vow
without words but with a shading of your eye
softening into an injured decision not
to inhale again the fumes of society.
Your eye is like the eye of a dog
I met as a child. I felt it was about
to speak to me the wisdom I would need
for my whole life, *if only it would talk.*
Yet understanding nothing would be spoken
made me vow to pledge my life to it.

A Second Bud

When anticipation fizzes from our roots,
We're not able to help how it loots our reason.
We can't tamp down its power—
something's going to happen!
We feel our brains about to flower.
Oh, it can lead to disappointment, of course.
Sometimes all the energy we put toward
the imaginary orchid of our reward
fizzles simply from being brought forward.
But is something dead in the bud so frightening
that we won't allow ourselves another goal?
A second bud, as a week runs its course,
inches unseen through the stem of each day.

Warrior Pose

Blades fly from our arms in yoga class,
fingers vibrating from the stretch.
But are we ready?
Even though the blades are imaginary,
they throw us off balance, and we are less
brave warriors than if we stayed on the couch,
curled up balls, unprepared.
How can we think ourselves into the full bloom
of power and vigilance? Perhaps
by imagining buds curled in our palms,
opened by the ants of persistence
and fed by new focus into peony flowers,
huge, magenta and smothering our enemy's
surprised face with lunging beauty.

Vita Poetica

To hook a finger in a loop you've found
after clawing and clawing at the cloth
of the universe collapsing around
your face like a parachute's vast moth wings,
alive, alive, but smothering until
you drag and pull, thinking your fingerbones
will crack with the effort; and then to fill
your nostrils with air, as the nether zones
of your organs fill with air,

                            means to grip
the overwhelming—the huge, the cloudy,
the suffocatingly monumental—
what you yourself may have blown up all
out of proportion and which now like whipped
silk spins at your feet until it vanishes,
leaving you upright, reborn in a *me*.
Oh, you may look the same, but inside, astonished
by what almost crushed you, now you begin:

Our Waking

after Roethke

I sleep to wake and take my waking fast.
I feel our fate in everything I fear.
I learn by knowing that we'll never last.

What makes me think I can escape the past?
I hear hysteria shift into gear.
I sleep to wake and take my waking fast.

You so close beside me, are you aghast?
Goddamn the ground! I stamp it madly here.
And learn, by forcing, that we'll never last.

Dark takes the city. Then the blast.
The worm descends a twisting stair.
You sleep. I wake—and take my waking fast.

Great Nature makes another protoplast,
a seed for you and me in dampened air.
We've learned by fearing that we'll never last.

This quaking keeps us steady. It's our ballast.
What rises up is always. But is far.
We've learned by knowing nothing ever lasts.
We sleep. We wake—and see our waking's vast.

First Blush

A freak spring snowstorm makes us take the old
route along a creek that flushes, gushes, touches
off tremors of foaming water so cold
and bright we know we've come to a source,
the beginning rush of a water's course
that later will slake the thirst of millions—
but now we are alone with it and know
its potential. Possibility plays before us.
It fizzes and spills up through consciousness,
rolling its April of yeses through groves
it will melt by noon, forcing
a green through the naked fields, through *us*.

Purr Riddle

Sound beneath layers of tissue and blood.
Marbles under a wash of water. Gush.
A percolating. Sound of a small god
exercising. Blood rising to a blush.
Louder if the listener is deaf, or
numb to rushes of feeling. What, in the hush
at twenty minutes after the hour,
we hear: the interior jungle. Lush
partings into partings into partings
of leaves revealing the rolling path to
the pulse's interior. All organs
working. The sound of well-being starting
and continuing, the full flesh clock, true
to its pledge—now-were, now-were—is our purr.

Pedicure

I was born for slaughter,
but in the abattoir I bolted
and escaped as the rough gate slid.
Only he came with me.
Now, high above the city,

I traipse through the living room
with my dripping watering can
toward the screen to the balcony garden,
past his face, flushed
in excitement at his book,

and glance down at my ankle
as I slide the screen open,
and notice the cleft remains of my hoof,
carved and painted as toes in my sandals,
and bend down to look for

a streak of blood or fecal matter
from the fear at what I saw
and how it all streamed from me
however many showers, baths, pumicings,
scrubbings, clippings, waxings,

massages and pedicures I have received.
The painted colors of my painted toes
rhyme with the colors of the annuals
cascading across the balcony.
Only that smear I check for

as I balance my watering can,
then think, *Just let it go,* as he has,
and step up over the sill.

The Garden Giraffes

In a hotel room in Brussels I wound
yards of bubble wrap around two garden
ornaments, twin metal giraffes I found
looking up at me from the street. Pardon?
They hadn't really spoken—just a mind probe
from the spirit inanimate objects have.
One was missing an ear. A turn of the globe,
if their tails and spindly legs behaved,
and they'd be in Canada, never to see
their melancholy tinsmith artist maker,
who kissed them on their head-horns
as I paid. I don't know if they were happy
rusting in our garden, then in storage, reborn
on our new balcony. As their caretaker
I can't awake in them the feelings I pretend.
But sometimes form itself makes us content.

Our Minor Art

We make love better unobserved—not that
we'd ever throw the new cats off the bed.
We let them sit there, turning their backs,
but listening anyway. We don't move in bed
quite with the freedom we might without them,
but the fact that they stay is like being
visited by minor gods. And we love the minor.
It inspires us because we like being
close to its genius—something we might come
to understand beyond our human bounds
but near to our kind—not like the major,
a capitalized God, for instance, or
uppercase Art. Those are beyond us,
yet our transformation here in bed is art,
something best made unobserved, even by the cats,
who leap off as we forget them and ourselves.

Quick Kiss

He sat at the table, then rose, day-wise,
as if off into life, but stopped to lean
over me as I raised my lips to say good-bye.

Suddenly he tilted my face down
and stamped my brow. It was an arc of love
inverted. It seemed to come down
from the sky and vanish into me,
as into a pool.

              Now beside the pool
grows a grafted tree.
In the dropped seed of a second gone by
he blessed me.

The Silver It Always Is

What if we imagine loss as being
overcome with the urge to give everything
away? There, now we have a shape for filling.
Hold on, let's not fill it with the same thing.
Let's wait for the shape of that emptiness
to soften, as arms loosen their embrace,
as clothes loosen, as lips part to confess
then reconsider and curve in the face
of what won't come back—not a broad smile, simply
a change from the grim line, a small upturn, as
a leaf revealing its belly to a breeze
shows the silver color it always is,
except now we notice it and notice how the tree
is prepared to give everything away.

Marriage

I watch my husband at a party,
a shy boy become a man at ease at last.
Success freshens his face, the boy now free
to pass beneath his expressions
as if slipping under a fence.
I used to slip under a fence
to swim in a stream-fed pond
and laze in the water till shocked
and delighted by a cold spot I swam through.
That's what his face is like,
infused by a source inside him.
I know I have a part in it,
just as I was part of the pond
where I loved to swim.

The Flaw

The best thing about a hand-made pattern
is the flaw.
Sooner or later in a hand-loomed rug,
among the squares and flattened triangles,
a little red nub might soar above a blue field,
or a purple cross might sneak in between
the neat ochre teeth of the border.
The flaw we live by, the wrong color floss,
now wreathes among the uniform strands
and, because it does not match,
makes a red bird fly,
turning blue field into sky.
It is almost, after long silence, a word
spoken aloud, a hand saying through the flaw,
I'm alive, discovered by your eye.

acknowledgments

The Canadian Broadcasting Corporation (CBC) commissioned the following poems: "Little Scar" and "The Silver It Always Is."

"The Cliffs of Mistake" in an early version was letterpress printed and hand-colored in a limited edition by Mindy Belloff at Intima Press.

"Gargoyle" was issued as a limited edition broadside by The Poetry Center of Chicago under the title "Celtic Lady Sex Gargoyle."

The following poems originally appeared, sometimes in earlier versions, in these literary journals, e-journals, or anthologies:

Black Warrior Review: "Artichoke Heart" (under the title "Artichoke Head"), "Fellini the Cat," "Good Fortune," "The Garden Giraffes," "Quick Kiss" (under the title "The Pool of Sky"), "Purr Riddle," "The Rescuer," "The Throne," (under the title "The Throne of Fear") and "Widow"

Boulevard: "Chance" (under the title "My Posthumous Wish"), "Of Night," "Old Friends" (under the title "Gently Waiting"), "Small Fry" (under the title "The Fish"), and "Vita Poetica" (under the title "The Poem")

Chance of a Ghost: An Anthology of Ghost Poems: "Great-Grandmother's Young Ghost" (under the title "Ghost in a Rocking Chair")

Cincinnati Review: "The Silver Arrow" and "The Vow"

The Cortland Review: "First Blush" (under the title "Enthusiasm")

Hampton Sydney Review: "Our Waking" and "Teacup Manifesto"

Margie: "The Blanket" and "In the Winter Dark" (under the title "Two Men by the Car")

Michigan Quarterly Review: "The Cliffs of Mistake" and "The Cup"

Ms. Magazine: "Ferocity in a Dishpan"

The National Poetry Review: "A Second Bud" (under the title "Anticipation")

North American Review: "Our Xanadu" (under the title "My Xanadu")

On Retirement, University of Iowa Press: "Drawing for Absolute Beginners"

Poetry Calendar 2008: "First Blush" (under the title "The Blush")

Prairie Schooner: "The Pearl Tear" and "Pink Paperclip"

The Raintown Review: "Blasphemy and Blame"

River Styx: "The Flaw," "The Fly" (under the title "The Swatter"), and "The Match"

Runes: "The End of the World" (under the title "The Sleigh")

Southwest Review: "The Happy Diary" and "Vision in the Backseat of a Taxi"

Storie Magazine (Italy): "Picnic" (under the title "The All of It")

Studio Online (Canada): "Pedicure"

TLS (*Times Literary Supplement*, UK): "Our Minor Art"

A Visit to the Gallery, Michigan University Press: "Girl and Friends View Naked Goddess"

notes

"Old Friends" is dedicated to Phillis Levin.

"First Blush" is dedicated to Thelma Rosner.

"Teacup Manifesto" refers to John Morris's front-page photograph in the *New York Times*, January 18, 2007.

and thanks

To Phillis Levin, always, for helping shape this book; to my editor Carol Houck Smith; to my agent Kathleen Anderson; to Annie Finch and to Georgianna Orsini for invaluable suggestions; to journal editors who've supported my work: Richard Burgin at *Boulevard,* Laurence Goldstein at *Michigan Quarterly Review,* Richard Newman at *River Styx,* and the editors at *Black Warrior Review*, Molly Dodd and Molly Oberlin; to James Cummins and John Drury at the University of Cincinnati for my time as Elliston Poet-in-Residence; to Sena Jeter Naslund, Kathleen Driskell, Karen Mann, and Katy Yocum at Spalding University; to Jean Feraca, host of the Poetry Circles on *Here on Earth*, Wisconsin Public Radio; and to my husband, Michael Groden, to whom this book is dedicated and who still deserves more thanks.

about the author

Molly Peacock is the author of six volumes of poetry, including *Cornucopia: New and Selected Poems*, as well as a memoir, *Paradise, Piece by Piece*, and a book about poetry, *How to Read a Poem and Start a Poetry Circle*. Her poems appear in leading periodicals and anthologies, including *The Best of the Best American Poetry* and *The Oxford Book of American Poetry*. She is the editor of a collection of essays on privacy, *The Private I: Privacy in a Public World* and coeditor of *Poetry in Motion: 100 Poems from the Subways and Buses*. Peacock is also the writer of and actor in a one-woman show in poems, *The Shimmering Verge*. A member of the Graduate Faculty of the Spalding University Brief Residency MFA Program in Creative Writing, she lives with her husband, Michael Groden, in Toronto, where she is Poetry Editor of the *Literary Review of Canada*.